The Smart Cı

How to Buy & Sell and Make Extra Money on Craigslist

Steve Johnson

Contents

Introduction

The Internet is a wonderful thing. We can do our grocery or clothes shopping, search for a vacation, find a job, meet new people, we can even fall in love! Whatever we do these days, we do it online.

There are pros and cons to this constantly switched on way of life, but the Internet is more than an information superhighway, and can actually be used to make cash too.

Yes, by having a strong Internet connection and a little tech-savvy know-how, you can line your bank account either a little or a lot, depending upon your effort level.

You've no doubt heard of eBay. This is an action website which allows you to buy and sell new or used goods for low prices, but have you heard of Craigslist?

Craigslist differs in many different ways to eBay, not least because it's not only about buying and selling old junk, but it's also about advertising services, finding a job, and making cash at the same time. Want to know more? This book is going to give you all the information you need to know on making extra cash on Craigslist, as well as how to avoid the inevitable scams, how to maximize your sales potential, and how to get started from scratch.

First things first, however, you need to know the address!

We are talking about this place - www.craigslist.org

Depending upon where you are in the world, you will be redirected to your local area site and the language spoken in that region. You can change these settings, however, if you prefer to be more international!

What is Craigslist?

Craigslist began from humble seedlings, in San Francisco, and was founded by Craig Newmark and Jim Buckmaster. Craigslist is a classified ads listing site, but the beauty is that you can list quickly and easily, and reach out to countless people in the process. This isn't the same as posting an ad in a local newspaper and hoping someone will read it - in this case, many people will read it!

The site's main job is to act as a host for those advertisements, organizing each is into set categories. Craigslist isn't just about goods to buy and sell, as we mentioned before, it can also be used for services, personal ads, and jobs. The site might look very simple in its design, but this is to allow people to find their way around it much more easily, rather than being dazzled by all singing, all dancing graphics and navigation menus. The simple nature is what makes Craigslist stand out amongst the ad world too.

If you want to enter into the forums, you can do so, and ask questions about items you want to purchase, sell, or anything you're looking for. There is a wealth of information to be found within these forums, and you can be assured of total safety in terms of your identity too.

To give you an idea of how quickly Craigslist has grown, the company began in one city in the USA, and now it covers countless countries and regions across the world, it contains in excess of 25 million classified ads at any one time and more than 1.5 million new postings for jobs. The forums are very active, with around 75 million posts, and it ranks amongst the world's top 10 sites in terms of page views. Basically, if you don't find what you're looking for on Craigslist, you're probably not going to find it at all!

Navigating Craigslist

We already mentioned that Craigslist is a very simple site in terms of its appearance, which is a completely intentional design technique. We are going to go into much more detail in a later chapter about how to actually use Craigslist, but for now, we need to talk about how to find your way around it.

It's a good idea to have your laptop, phone, or tablet close to you whilst reading this book, so you can look at the site at the same time. This will increase your understanding hugely.

If you want to simply look at the site, you can do so without registering, but if you want to actually do anything, e.g. buy something, post a listing, or take part in a forum discussion, you will need to register and sign up to be a member. This is free, and a quick and easy process.

You will see that the listings are organized into categories, and then subcategories. This is designed to make it easier for you to find exactly what you're looking for, rather than scrolling through endless ads for things you have no interest in. For example, you will find a category 'for sale'. If you search within that category you will find subheadings, e.g. furniture, free, garage sale, jewelry, etc. This helps you spend less time searching and more time focused on what you really need.

This book is focused on selling on Craigslist, and therefore making some cold, hard cash from the Internet. You can easily sell the things you no longer want, having a good, old clear out of your garage or home, and decluttering, whilst making cash. It is also worth pointing out and being aware that you can purchase whatever you want from Craigslist, as well as find jobs and services too. Before you read on, have a good, detailed look through the site and browse the various categories. This will give you a basis on which to understand further what we're going to talk about.

Craigslist isn't a difficult site to use, and the mechanics behind it are actually really simple. What you need to be aware of however is a few hidden pieces of information, which will take your sales from 'good', to 'fantastic'. If you know these hints and tips, you'll be able to make more cash than you probably ever realized!

Chapter 1: Why Should You Sell on Craigslist?

Is your home or garage full of junk? Do you have a wardrobe full of clothes that you no longer wear? Are you keen to have an early spring clean and declutter your home?

If you're nodding your head, then you have three main options:

- You can throw it out
- You can donate it to a charity shop
- You can list it on Craigslist and make a profit

The fact you are reading this book tells us that you are firmly in the third option's camp and you want to make some money. Great choice.

In our introduction we talked about what Craigslist is, where it came from, and what you can do with it, but why should you choose Craigslist over other auction and selling sites? eBay is hugely popular and offers a lot of buyer protection, so why should you shun the auction giant and go with Craig instead?

Basically, Craigslist has a few advantages over the other main auction sites online.

Advantages of Using Craigslist to Sell Items

Exactly why should you use Craigslist? Here are a few reasons.

- **No Need to Package and Ship** - If you've ever used eBay in the past, you'll know the euphoria of selling an items quickly diminishes when you have to start packaging up the item, taking it to the post office, having it weighed, shipping it, taking account of shipping costs from what you sold it for, and then praying it gets there in one piece. It's a pain and it takes time and effort. Whilst you factor in the cost of packaging to the price, it doesn't take away the fact that sometimes the shipping price ends up being more, and you lose out. With Craigslist you don't have this issue, because the listing is local. This means you take the item to the person, either by a meet up, or they come to collect from you. We will cover the safety aspects in terms of meet ups in a later chapter, but for now, not having to package up and ship is a major advantage.

- **Easy to Use the Site** - Craigslist is deliberately simple in appearance and in usage. This means anyone can use it, literally anyone. Whilst posting an ad is a little more time consuming than simply searching for something to buy, it is by no means difficult. Once your ad has been posted, you simply sit back and wait for someone to contact you who is interested in purchasing your item. You communicate back and forth, arrange everything and bingo! Sale made!

- **Customer Service Back up** - If you notice you have an issue with a buyer or a seller, you can easily contact customer support for help and advice. Generally speaking, Craigslist staff do not get involved in sales unless there is an issue, but knowing that they're there for you if need be, is a weight off the mind.

- **A Very Convenient Service** - The fact that ads on Craigslist are local means you don't have to deal with time zones and differences, and no misunderstandings in general. The convenience of being able to reach out to a wider number of people means your sale is more likely to be successful too.

- **Your Email Address Isn't Visible** - When you place a posting and communicate with a potential buyer, your email address is kept secret. This takes away the possible worry about privacy issues.

- **It's Free to Place a Listing** - You don't need to pay for your listings, unlike on eBay. There are some anomalies to this point, e.g. if you are posting a job advert, a property advert or a service, but if you're simply selling items, the listing is totally free. This means you can make money on your sales, compared to other auction sites who may take a large percentage cut of the sale.

What Can You Sell on Craigslist?

Basically anything, within reason!

Currently, the sub-categories for sales are:

- Antiques
- Appliances
- Arts & crafts
- Atv/utv/sno
- Auto parts
- Aviation
- Baby & Kid
- Barter
- Beauty & health
- Bike parts
- Bikes
- Boat parts
- Boats
- Books
- Business
- Cars & trucks
- Cds/DVD/VHS
- Cell phones
- Clothes & accessories
- Collectibles
- Computer parts
- Computers
- Electronics
- Farm & garden
- Free
- Furniture
- Garage sale
- General
- Heavy equipment
- Household
- Jewelry
- Materials
- Motorcycle parts
- Motorcycles
- Music instruments
- Photo & Video
- RVS & camping
- Sporting
- Tickets
- Tools
- Toys & Games

- Trailers
- Video gaming
- Wanted
- Wheels & Tires

As you can see, there is plenty of scope in there for whatever you want to sell! This list should give you some idea of the types of things you might have lurking in your house or garage that you could list on Craigslist and potentially make some cash from. If you don't find your category on that list, there is always the 'general' sub-category, but do be aware that the more specific you can be in terms of which category you list your item in, the greater the chance of making a sale.

For most people, the answer to 'why sell your items on Craigslist' is about decluttering and cash. Those are two fantastic reasons to go with but remember that you can use Craigslist to find a job, access services, and speak to people on the forums too. The more sales you make, the more you are likely to use Craigslist for your other endeavors too. Familiarizing yourself with the site, working slowly, and listing one thing at a time for the first few times you use it, will help you to streamline your selling and avoid any potential pitfalls.

Whilst Craigslist is very easy to use, a sale isn't definite until you have traded cash for the item, and in-between that time, communication breakdowns and issues can easily derail your profit-making efforts!

Chapter 2: Can You Actually Make Money on Craigslist?

The reason we are writing this book is simply that the answer to that question is a very large 'yes'!

At first, you cannot expect to get rich from Craigslist, but that really does depend on what you have to sell and how you sell it. You should begin by having a clear out and selling the things you do not need anymore. There is no use in hoarding items if you don't use them - if that item hasn't seen the light of day for the last year and it has no sentimental value to you, get it listed!

There are two ways you can make cash from Craigslist:

• Selling items you already have, which you no longer need
• Reselling in-demand items for a profit

Later on in the book, we are going to talk about hints and tips to maximize sales, and we're also going to talk about how to list an item properly, but for now, these are the things you need to know which could affect how much cash you make from your Craigslist sales.

Selling the items you have in your house which you no longer need is the quickest and easiest way to make money from the site, but as you become more familiar with it, and the more you successfully sell, you might like to take a step further. There are many professional sellers on sites like Amazon and eBay, and you can do the same with Craigslist if you put in the time and effort to find the items which are in demand, which sell for a good price, and which are easy to source.

For instance, you could go into the cell phone case business (a very in-demand area, but just as an example). This means you would look at how much cell phone cases were selling for and how much they cost to buy, check if there is a real saturation of the market in your area or whether there is space for you too, and then purchase some in, or buy when you need, and sell on for a greater profit. You could easily use this as a passive income method!

So, where to start?

Identify The Item And The Right Price

It's a good idea to identify the item you want to sell and then head online and do some research on how much it would cost to buy it new. Obviously, if you're selling things you already have in your home, you shouldn't try and sell the item for the brand-new price, because your item is second hand and therefore the cost needs to be lower. What you can do is use other auction sites and find similar items, and see how much they are selling for there. This gives you a good guideline on how much to ask for, and will avoid overcharging, or even worse, losing out on money yourself by undercharging!

If the item has any defects, e.g. any chips, breakages, or anything else cosmetically or mechanically wrong with it, you will need to list this, and the price will need to be lower to reflect this defect. This is something to bear in mind. Never list something as being in perfect condition if it isn't. You will be caught out and your sale will not go ahead. Be honest at all times. Look at it this way, you wouldn't want the same to happen to you, would you?

Identify Your Niche Interest

If you really want to go down the line of selling on Craigslist on a regular basis, you need to identify the niche you're going to work with. It's no good jumping from one area to another, as you're simply going to confuse yourself, and you cannot become an expert in every single selling area! It's best to specialize in one or two niches, e.g. the cell phone case example we just mentioned, and you could then branch out into laptop cases in the future.

By understanding how in demand your niche is and the prices you can expect to buy and sell for, you can see whether or not you have chosen the right area, or whether you would be better to switch areas and find greater profits elsewhere. Making money from Craigslist might not happen overnight, so do be prepared to learn about the niche you want to specialize in properly and understand how to price each item realistically. When you communicate with customers, they want to know that they are dealing with someone who is genuine and who understands what they are trying to sell. This will reduce the chances of a sale falling through.

How to Register on Craigslist

Once you've decided you want to go ahead and sell items on Craigslist, you will need to register for a free account. This enables you to sell items, buy items, and use the forums. Registering is free, very quick, and very easy.

When registering you simply click 'my account' on the main page. This will then take you to a page which asks for your log in details, or it will ask you to 'create account'. In order to create your account, you simply need to enter your email address. Once you have done this will you be sent a verification email, which you simply need to click to verify you are indeed who you say you are!

That's it! You are now registered to buy, sell, and use the forums on Craigslist.

You can post your item for free, and you do not pay any fees if you sell it. That's the major upside of Craigslist, compared to other auction sites, such as eBay. Do be aware, however, if you want to post a job listing, a property listing, or you want to post about a service, you will need to pay fees, but for the purposes of this book we are talking about selling items, so those fees shouldn't really apply to you.

Chapter 3: The Correct Way to Sell on Craigslist

Now you've decided that you want to use Craigslist to make some cash, it's time to find out exactly how to go about selling things correctly, in order to ensure success comes your way. Again, a little later we're going to dedicate a whole chapter to tips on maximizing your sales, but in this chapter, we will take about the main areas to bear in mind, in order to make your first sale.

Remember to go ahead and register for your free account before you even start trying to work towards selling anything on Craigslist. It is quick, easy, and free, and as soon as you're set up, you're good to go. This also gives you access to the forums which are a great source of information within the site. You can go on here and read threads, and if you want to take part in a conversation you can; if you just want to read and soak up some knowledge, you can do that too!

Let's go through a step by step guide on how to make sure you sell your item, or items, correctly on Craigslist.

How to Sell Your Item

Identify Your Item And Make Sure it is Suitable

We talked in our last chapter about finding things within your home or garage which you don't want anymore, and this is the ideal place to start. What you need to find out however is whether the item you want to sell is suitable. Does it work? Are there too many cosmetic defects with it? If so, it's not the best idea to try and sell it and your effort will be wasted. If however, there is nothing wrong with it mechanically, or to a degree, and it looks great, you can go ahead and list it.

Remember to look through the categories we talked about in our last chapter. If you identify the right category, as close to your item as possible, then you have more chance of a sale. The reason for this is because when someone is searching for a particular item to buy, they will be as direct as possible. This means they will look in the category which makes the most sense, and if it's not there, they're not likely to go searching through loose-fitting categories. It's a little like the search results you see on Google - most people only look at the first page, the second page if they're lucky, but they do not really go beyond that. Category choosing is the same kind of process, so make sure you're as specific as you can possibly be. If you're not too sure, spend some time browsing, to get a clearer idea of where the item should go.

For instance, a gel nail lamp would go under beauty and health, a car engine would go under car parts, etc.

Choosing The Correct Price

Now you know what you want to sell and you know which category fits it best, you need to come up with a fair price. This price needs to be attractive enough to gain attention and make people want to buy your product, but it also needs to be high enough to make the sale worth your time. If you go too low, you're sure to sell your item quite probably, but you'll lose out on its worth. If you go too high, nobody is going to think your item is worth buying, because they can probably go out and buy a new version for the same, or very similar. It's a fine line to walk!

The best advice, as before, is to do some research online into how much the item retails for when new, and then look online at other auction sites to see how much it sells for second hand. Come to a good piece of middle ground, which not only covers your profit but also doesn't take the price too far away from being attractive to the buyer. Research is key in this regard and will be the difference between a sale, and no cash coming your way at all.

Take Quality Photographs

If you list your item without a photograph it is extremely unlikely to sell. For that reason, you need to take a very good photo of the item you're selling and you also need to photograph any defects that are part of the sale. These need to be added to the description, but a visual is always better for helping the buyer to understand just how bad/minimal the defect is.

Hopefully there will be no defect and in that case, you can simply go ahead and photograph the item in the best possible light, without any distractions in the background. The more professional your photo looks, this will increase the chances of the buyer trusting you as a seller. Obviously, make sure the item is clean and in the best possible state as you take a photo of it!

The more photos you can include in your listing, the better. Most people tend to buy items which have more than one photo, but at the very least make sure you have one very high-quality photo of the item. If you are going to add in more than one image, you should take photos from different sides, so the buyer has plenty of information on the visual side of the item you're trying to sell.

Create a Clear Headline

The headline is basically the name of the item you're trying to sell, so don't be too obscure and be as direct and clear as possible. If you are selling a gel nail lamp, call it a gel nail lamp, and don't go too far into specifics, e.g. a UV thermal nail heating machine! Stick to basics, as that is what people will search for when they browse the site for the items they want to buy the most.

By making your item easy to be searched for, it will appear in search results much more often, and as a result, you are much more likely to make a sale. The specifics of the item will then be outlined in the description, which we'll come onto shortly. If the item is sub-standard, e.g. part of it doesn't work, it's up to you whether you highlight this in the headline, or whether you leave that until the description. This is a grey area in many ways because if the reader sees anything about it not working in tip-top condition, they're probably going to flick over to the next item. If however, you catch their attention with the first headline and then give them the information in more detail in the description, they may still be inclined to buy it. For that reason, perhaps leave it until the description.

Write a Clear And Helpful Description

This is where you get to sell your item in the best possible light. The description shouldn't be too long, as you don't want to bore potential buyers, but it needs to give them all the information they need. For that reason, consider using bullet points to outline the features of the product. The description should contain:

- The name and brand of the item
- The age of the item
- The working order, e.g. if there is any defect, and the details if so
- Any accessories included with the product
- Is it in the original packaging/box?
- Any item specifics which you feel are necessary, but keep this brief
- Features, in a bullet point list (if necessary)

The description shouldn't be too sales-like, and instead should be clear and polite. Also, make sure that the format of your description is easy to read, and that the potential buyer can skim read the main details if necessary, rather than having large paragraph blocks of text. This is another reason why bullet points work well.

Decide How You Want People to Contact You

You can leave either your email, your telephone number, or you can enter both. It is best to include your phone number because that way you are more likely to make a sale. The reason is that people still like to pick up the phone and call quickly; they think if they do this, they are going to get in there before anyone else, as their email could be lost within your inbox quite easily. If you don't want to leave your phone number, that's also fine, but be aware that you might make potential buyers contacting you slightly less likely.

If you are only going to leave your email, make sure you check your inbox on a regular basis, so you don't keep people waiting for replies.

Sell Your Item!

From there, you're ready to submit your item and wait for buyers to start messaging or calling you. It might take a while, it might be instant, so it's important to be patient and not to become obsessed with checking every five minutes! Having said that, keep your inbox within sight, as we mentioned before.

Clean Your Item and Box it

It's a good idea, whilst you're waiting for buyers to contact you, to clean up the item and box it up, ready for collection. You do not have to package your item in the same way you would if you were selling your item on eBay, but you do want to make it easy for the person to carry the item away from your ownership, e.g. in a box or a large bag. Make sure you clean your item well, ready for the sale to be completed.

Points to Remember When Listing Your Item

Listing an item for sale on Craigslist is quite easy, and provided you have all the information to hand, it shouldn't take you too long. If you need more information on the features of the product, you can always research this online and use the details you find. The most important thing to remember is to always be honest and not to stretch the truth when it comes to the quality of your item or any of the features.

If you want to avoid problems after the sale has gone through, you need to make sure that you tell the truth. Look at it this way - would you want to buy something, pay money, get it home and then realize that it isn't what you were promised at all? Of course not! In this case, always be honest with the listing details and if there are any problems or defects with it, it's best to speak up at this point, then deal with the issues later on. A product which has a few cosmetic issues or a defect isn't necessarily going to not sell, and it's often the case that people are happy to accept a slightly sub-standard product, as long as the price reflects that.

Also make sure that your description is easy to scan, easy to read, and has the right friendly and polite tone. You are not a store trying to sell something online, so avoid overly sales-focused language.

Overall, be aware of the following points:

- Be honest and open about the product
- Make your description easy to read
- Don't make the description too long
- Don't overprice or underprice the product

- Check your contact details before listing the product
- Clean the product well, in anticipation of the sale

Once you are contacted by a potential buyer, make sure you answer in a timely manner, to avoid them becoming tired of waiting, and therefore you miss out on the cash!

Chapter 4: Safety And Meet Ups

You've made a sale, congratulations!

The next thing you need to do is arrange to meet up to pass the item over or have the item collected from you. Of course, as with any type of meeting someone you don't know endeavor, you need to exercise caution and common sense. Do not simply give someone your home address and ask them to come over when you're home alone. You do not know this person. Whilst we would hope that they are perfectly fine and honest, you simply shouldn't take the risk.

We should point out that the overwhelming majority of sales on Craigslist are conducted completely professionally and there are rarely any problems, but your safety is not something you should gamble with, so a few precautions and safeguards should be put in place.

How to Receive Money Safely

When making a sale on Craigslist, you have two options in terms of being paid:

- In cash
- Via PayPal

The single best way to receive the money from your Craigslist sale is by cash when the person collects the item. You could use PayPal also, and we'll cover that in a second. Never give someone your bank details and ask them to deposit the money. You might think this is quicker and easier, but giving someone your personal bank details is risky, and you do not know who you are dealing with!

Of course, you should not give the item to anyone without receiving the cash at the same time. For this reason, meetups or collections should always be along the lines of 'here is the money', and then 'here is the item'.

This is also something you should point out to the buyer when you are speaking to them before the sale is finalized. This cuts down on any confusion and ensures that the sale goes through much quicker and easier than otherwise.

Should you accept payment by PayPal? This is another possibility, because it is usually linked to your home email address, and the banking side of things is anonymous. If the amount of cash is large, or the person simply doesn't want to draw out the cash and bring it to you, you could ask them to deposit the correct amount prior to you giving them the item, and that gives you time to check the money goes through properly. If there are any delays with the deposit being made, e.g. the funds are held before crediting to your account, wait to give them the item until the delay is cleared up.

How you are going to receive the money is something you should talk about with the buyer when you are communicating back and forth, and it is important to be clear on arrangements from the start. Never accept payment from anyone who makes it difficult, e.g if they are asking for bank details and not willing to deviate from their wishes, or they are asking if payment can be made from a source which you simply don't feel right about.

There are some strange people out there! That's not to say you're going to meet one, but it's important to be careful in terms of checking that you actually receive the money, before you hand over the item. Remember, you can always try and sell again, but if you hand it over and don't get paid, you're completely out of pocket.

Meet Ups And Collection Tips

The fact you are meeting someone you do not know means you need to exercise caution, and this means using your common sense above everything else. Of course, not everyone you sell items to on Craigslist is going to threaten your safety, but it pays to always be on your guard!

How you pass the item to the buyer depends on a few things, mainly on whether or not you drive, and how badly you actually want to make the sale. If you drive, life gets a little easier, as that means you can arrange a mutually convenient point to make the sale, i.e. in public. If you don't drive, that means you're going to have to use public transport to get to your meeting point, which could be time-consuming and it's also going to cost you money in terms of bus/train fares. The point you meet at has to be convenient for you both, but possibly more so for you because this shouldn't be costing you any money!

Here are a few tips for arranging meetups and collections for items you sell on Craigslist.

Never Arrange Collections From Home

Your safety is vital, so never arrange for the item to be collected from your home, or from someone else's home. Giving your address out is not a good idea, and you don't know who is going to be turning up at your door. They may not even be alone. In this case, arranging a meeting point is always a better option. If the buyer presses to collect the item from your home because it's quicker, explain that you are often out, at work, etc, and make your excuses. If they still won't budge from their request, it's best to try and sell to someone else. Yes, you might miss out on the sale, but what is their reason for being so adamant on visiting your house? That is something you have to ask yourself.

Always Meet in Public

Choose a meeting point which is in a public space, e.g. a shopping mall, a coffee shop, or a restaurant. Never arrange to meet up in a car park or somewhere which is a relatively desolate area. Keep in mind that you need people milling around you in order to create a sense of safety for you. Of course, meeting in public is also a matter of safety for the buyer too, as whilst we're focusing on the fact that you don't know them, they don't know you either! Keeping the process in the public eye will protect you both and make you both feel easier and assured about the sale going through to completion successfully.

Day Time is Better

Meeting in the daytime is always better than meeting at night or when the night is falling. Again, this is a matter of safety and being seen in public, and it also makes the meeting process easier because you can see each other! If you meet in the dark, you can easily miss one another and this is going to make the delivery process harder.

Mid-afternoon or mid-mornings are good times to meet, as they're convenient for most people and these are also busy times in public places. If the weather is particularly bad, e.g. very heavy rain which is making visibility difficult or making the day seem strangely dark, rearrange the collection and meet another time. Not only will your buyer probably not want to head out in the rain, but dark conditions are simply not safe for you either.

Be Flexible in Order to Confirm Safety

It's important to come to a mutually convenient time and place for both of you, but there may be times when this is difficult, e.g. due to work or family commitments. The best advice is to do your very best in terms of making the collection process as quick and easy as possible. It isn't going to take more than five minutes maximum for the handing over of the cash and the item, so if it is possible to quickly head out of work on a break, you could do that. It's always best to put yourself out in terms of rushing a little, rather than trying to meet someone in a time which is deemed unsafe. Safety has to come first, and this is something which should come over and above your eagerness to make a sale.

Chapter 5: The Smart Way to Buy

We've talked so far about selling items on Craigslist and making cash from it, but if we flip the coin to the opposite side, it's entirely possible to save money by buying on Craigslist too! There are some real bargains to be found, and if you're looking for something obscure or something you're struggling to find in stores, you might very well find someone having a clear out and selling the item you've been looking for.

As with selling, there are a few things you need to bear in mind, and a few safety considerations to think about too. Familiarizing yourself with the site and how it all works before you start to buy anything is vital. You might have been looking at the site from a seller's point of view to date, but buying is a slightly different area. Being aware of the site from all angles will help you to avoid any pitfalls, and find the biggest bargains around.

Why Buy From Craigslist?

We've talked in detail throughout the book to date about why you should sell your unwanted items on Craigslist, and why you should even think about purchasing goods to resell on, but what about buying - why should you purchase items from Craigslist?

Everyone out there has been doing the same as you to date - they have been having household clear outs and they're trying to sell the things they no longer want for a little extra cash. There is nothing particularly worrying or offhand about that, and provided you do your research into what you're buying, you could find yourself with a serious bargain in your midst.

The main advantages of buying from Craigslist are:

- You can find items for sale which are probably not in the shops
- You can arrange your price to a certain degree, so you save cash and grab some bargains
- You are able to browse the site when it suits you, so your purchases are convenient

- Sales are done locally, so you don't have to worry about shipping and possible delays
- You can ask questions about the item and make sure it is really what you're looking for

Let's take antiques, for example. Whilst there are many antique dealers out there, finding the one pieces you've been searching years for can be a case of luck. Someone has found an item in their garage and they have no clue what it is. It was handed down to them by a member of the distant family and they simply want to get rid of it because it's cluttering the place up and collecting dust. That item is the piece you've been searching for and because the buyer doesn't really have a lot of antique knowledge, you can purchase it for a lower price than if you went to an expert dealer.

Most people on Craigslist aren't trying to make the world's biggest profit, they're simply trying to sell their items for a fair price. This means great items for you, at low prices.

Tips For Buying on Craigslist

Don't Just Buy For The Sake of It

It's very easy to sit at home with your laptop, browsing shopping sites, and thinking 'oh, I'll buy that!' What you need to do is ask yourself if you really need it. If you do, go for it; if you're simply making impulse buys, it's probably going to end up back on Craigslist at a later date, when you have a household clear out too!

Only purchase items that you are very sure you want, and be prepared to go through the process of contacting the buyer, arranging the collection, and actually going to pick up the item and hand over the cash. Don't be a time waster, and don't be someone who purchases for the sake of it and then wishes they didn't!

Is it a Good Deal or Not?

It really depends on what you're buying, but is the item really that good of a deal? This is where you need to do some research into prices and specifics before you make contact with the buyer and express an interest. The reason many people bypass this stage is that they're so keen to get in there first and not miss out on purchasing the item, that they rush trying to find out what they're getting themselves into. Don't worry about missing out - if you're supposed to get it, you will, and it's always better to give yourself an extra half an hour of research time than end up buying an item for much more than its worth in the end.

Head online and look at other auction sites, to discover how much the same item is being sold for elsewhere. Also look at the cost of buying the item brand new, and work out whether or not the asking price is fair, or even low enough to consider snapping their hand off.

Negotiate But Don't Lowball Someone

It is entirely possible and probably expected that you try and negotiate the price. If you're selling an item, this is going to happen to you, and it's always better to try and work with the buyer than simply say 'no'. If they are asking for a ridiculously low price, of course, you are well within your rights to refuse, but it's a good idea to consider other offers.

When you find an item you want to buy and you've done your research into how much it should cost, message the seller and offer a slightly lower price. Do not lowball a seller, it's just not good sense. You wouldn't want someone to do the same thing to you, and quite frankly it's insulting. Whatever price you try and negotiate to, make sure it is fair for both of you. If your new offer is accepted, great, you've got yourself a bargain. If not, consider paying the asking price, or moving on.

Always be Polite

This goes without saying, but always be polite with a seller. You're more likely to clinch the sale if you're polite with them, rather than being someone who is asking far too many unnecessary questions, over-messaging, and offering insulting prices. Always put yourself in the shoes of the seller and consider their feelings at the same time. Remember, people selling on Craigslist are not in serious business, they are just people trying to sell their items and make a little cash!

Why Are They Selling?

If the item is being sold for a great price and the product is in fantastic condition, you really need to ask the question of why they are selling it in the first place. It's not rude to ask this question, and any seller should be prepared to hear it and answer it. It is quite likely that they're selling it because they simply don't need it anymore and it's taking up precious space in their house or garage. That's a fine and very viable excuse. On the other hand, the answer could set alarm bells in your mind, and that is when you probably need to take our next step and ask whether or not you can test out the item before parting with any cash.

Someone who seems overly-eager to sell an item for a low price, despite listing it as in tip-top condition with no mechanical issues, could be being a little less than honest about the item's condition.

Can You Try The Item Before You Buy it?

If you are parting with a large amount of cash, or the item is mechanical or very large, then you can ask if you can try the item out first. For instance, many people sell cars on Craigslist, and you're not going to hand over cash without looking it over in person first! The same goes for anything electronic - you need to know that it is working correctly before you commit 100% to buy it. If a seller says 'no' then you need to really be a little suspicious and ask yourself why.

An honest and open seller should have no problem with you trying the item out, and will help to make arrangements for that to happen. They might not want you to go to their house to test it out, and that's something you need to respect because it's about their safety, but they should make other arrangements instead.

Take Someone With You

If you are buying something large and you simply cannot meet in public, then always take someone with you when you go to collect or try out the product. Do not go alone as you have no idea where you are going, and who is going to be waiting for you when you arrive. Taking a trusted friend or family member with you, and letting someone else know where you are going, and the details of the address, is simply good safety sense, and something any self-respecting seller should expect you to be doing also. If the seller doesn't want you to go with another person, steer clear and cancel the sale. Alarm bells should ring in that case.

Buying items on Craigslist is a great way to find bargains, large items, and rare items. Provided you ask the right questions and check everything out before handing over the cash, you could find yourself with the item you've always wanted. Of course, buying items also gives you the opportunity to sell them on for a greater profit, so always be on the lookout for fantastic bargains too.

Chapter 6: How to Avoid Scams

We've talked a lot so far in this book not only about how to use Craigslist but also about safety. This isn't an accident - whilst Craigslist itself is a very safe site, the fact you are meeting up with and communicating with people you have never met before means you need to keep your guard up. This advice is certainly not only apparent with Craigslist, but with any buying and selling site which involves you meeting other people.

In addition to that, you need to careful about possible scams.

Wherever there are people, there are always going to be a mix of good and bad. This is something no site can stop from happening, and all you can do is be extra careful. We should point out that the huge majority of transactions on Craigslist are completely above board, legit, and very honest. The people who speak on forums are also 99% honest, open, and friendly, but there is always bound to be a very small minority who are out to ruin it for the rest.

Don't let them win, simply keep your wits about you and be educated on the possible scams that might be lurking out there.

Questions to Ask Yourself/Things to be Aware of

Is This Deal Too Good to be True?

It pays to be a little suspicious sometimes, and if you notice someone is selling a quality product for a rather low price, you need to ask yourself why. We have touched upon this already, but sometimes a seller is trying to offload a defect product for a better price, without giving you the real low down on the quality or status of the product.

You can easily get around this possible scam by asking the seller why they are actually selling the item. Their answer should tell you quite a lot, and you can also ask directly if there are any defects in the product. We're going to talk shortly about the tone of voice and language used but never distrust your gut. If you're asking these direct questions and they are hesitating or being overly defensive, there is probably something they're not telling you. Again, you can ask to try the product before you buy it also, but never go alone and always take someone else with you.

Listen to Your Gut

Do you trust the person and what they are telling you? Have a phone conversation with them and listen to their tone of voice. Whilst it's possible that the person is just shy and not great at speaking to strangers over the phone, there are some tell-tale signs which point towards rather shifty behavior. Signs to look out for include:

- Saying 'umm', 'ahh', 'err' a lot when you are asking direct questions they should know the answer to
- What is their tone of voice like? Are they speaking very fast? Do they sound nervous? These are signs that something might not be as it seems
- They are very vague on details. A person selling an item should know about what they're selling and should be able to answer all necessary questions
- They refuse to compromise on anything

At the end of the day, your gut will not let you down and if you're simply getting a feeling that something isn't quite right, it's best to pass on the sale and look for someone who is a little more upfront and honest. If you are the one doing the selling and it is a buyer who you're not quite sure about, there is nothing wrong with possibly telling the person that the item is no longer available. It is better to tell a little white lie and get yourself out of the situation than be forced to meet someone who you really aren't quite sure about. Again, safety is key.

Do They Give Their Telephone Number?

A scammer, whether a buyer or a seller, will not give you their telephone number and will insist only on email contact. It might also be the case that they don't want to be contacted via the regular email they have used to register for Craigslist, and they will ask you to message them via a different address, which is likely to look a little odd. This is because messages cannot be reached from the Craigslist point of view, once the communication is out of their registered address.

It is normal for some people not to want to give out their telephone number to people they don't know, and that is why this one is quite hard to manage. What you should do however is listen to what your gut says, and if that is screaming 'scam!', then you should listen.

Do They Ask For Other Payment Methods?

For your own safety and security only ever ask for cash or PayPal when buying or selling. Cash is always preferable, but there may be times when that is not possible. In that case, make sure the PayPal transaction has gone through and is registered on the transaction history as coming from the person making the purchase or sale before you hand over the item.

If the person is constantly asking for your bank details because they can't do it any other way, they don't have PayPal, or some other reason which you simply don't feel easy about, do not listen. Do not give your bank details out to anyone, especially someone you meet via a purchase or sale on Craigslist.

Avoid Buying or Selling Expensive Items at First

When you first start using Craigslist, it is best to start slow and low. Avoid making large cash sales or purchases until you have a little more Craigslist experience. There are some people out there who will take advantage of someone who seems to be inexperienced in using the site, and whilst you can fake confidence, these people are quite clever and know the signs to look for. Stick with low priced products at first and as your confidence and experience grow, you can use the site for larger and higher priced purchases.

Always Test Out Electronics

Electronics are probably the number on scam area, because these can be purchased from anywhere in the world, and could also be extremely fake. Unless you see it for yourself and test it out, you could be buying extremely substandard equipment and paying well over the odds for it. If they refuse to let you test it, shrug your shoulders and move on, because that is a sure fire sign of a scam.

The best advice when it comes to using Craigslist for the first few times is to simply be aware that there are scams out there and to be very careful. You will become more used to the things that are asked of you naturally, and the questions to put to a seller, but when you are new it's important to start slowly. Being suspicious of everyone might sound like a rather negative mindset, but it's best to be protective of yourself and your cash with people you just don't know.

Chapter 7: How to Get The Most From Craigslist

By this point in the book, you should be quite sure that there is a very real possibility to make cash from selling and reselling on Craigslist. What you need to know now, is how to maximize those sales and give yourself the very best chance of lining your bank account.

We have already touched upon some of the best tips already as we've moved through the various topics we have covered, but to give you a quick reference guide, here are some of the very best hints and tips to help you get the most from your sales on Craigslist.

Expect Offers, so Price Your Item a Little Higher

You might think this is contradictory because we've talked about giving prices which are in line with what else is offered online, but that doesn't mean that you can't be savvy and price your item around 2-3% higher. The reason is that buyers are likely to contact you and try and negotiate the price. If you put the price as what you've researched online, and then you negotiate with a prospective buyer, you're going to miss out. By placing the price around 3% higher maximum, you're giving yourself wiggle room, and you won't end up with a loss of profits.

Always Get The Category As Close as Possible

We have covered this one already but it is so vitally important we need to mention it again. When listing an item for sale, you need to choose the most accurate category possible. People do not eat to spend endless hours searching through every item for sale on the entirety of Craigslist in their region, so make life a little easier for them. If you're not sure, then do some more research, but the closest match you choose, the more likely it is that someone is going to find your item and contact you about buying it.

Focus on Your Headline

In terms of grabbing attention, your headline is the thing you need to focus on. By being as clear and simple as possible, you will attract more possible buyers your way. If you're too intricate and you use language which only an expert in that particular item would know, you're cutting out your chances of working with less than experts, or newbies to Craigslist. Stick to basics.

Check Your Contact Information!

Do you know how many people have listed an item on Craigslist and then wondered why nobody is contacting them? It's because they put the wrong phone number down, or they missed out a number in their email address! The most simple thing in the world, but double check your contact information before you list the item for sale and you will enhance your chances by a million!

Check The Area You're Registered in

Check that you are listing your item in the correct region. For instance, if you live in New York, make sure you are selling the item with the borough or few boroughs closest to your home. Unless you want to travel all the way across the New York state, this will eliminate the chances of selling an item, only for it to fall through when it comes to arranging collection.

Make Your Photographs High Quality

It's no good taking a blurry photograph of the item with your phone and expecting interest to come your way. The photos you take need to be high quality and they need to show all sides of the item. For that reason, consider posting more than one photo, especially if there are any defects or cosmetic issues.

Always Answer Queries

Surely this is obvious, but you should always answer questions which come your way via email or telephone. This person could be your new buyer, but if you're too busy to answer their email, or you just don't want to answer the phone right at that moment and forget to call back, you could miss the sale entirely. There is nothing to say that someone else is going to contact you instead, so always make sure you return calls and reply to emails. It's just polite if nothing else!

By knowing the tricks of the trade and being as open and honest as possible, you can easily maximize your potential Craigslist sales and make a tidy profit.

Conclusion

And there we have it! Your complete guide to making cash from Craigslist, either by clearing out your garage and selling on the items you no longer use, or actually buying items and reselling them for a profit. Whichever route you go down, having the expert knowledge on how to actually go about it will stand you in great stead.

Having a house or garage clear out is the ideal way to get started on Craigslist, but as your confidence grows, you could easily branch out into reselling. As we have mentioned, this means purchasing items and then selling them on for a profit. There are certain niches which are more popular than others for reselling, and the main ones are books, cellphones, cellphone accessories, and computer parts or hardware. These are the types of items which are often searched for on local selling sites, rather than purchasing them on large auction sites or new from online brands. You can usually find great bargains in this way, which is why most people will use sites such as Craigslist first and foremost.

Of course, that's not to say that you can't look at other niches, but it's vital to do your research beforehand. Take some time looking at the types of products which are already for sale and see how quickly they remain there, and how quickly the posting is taken down. Once the posting has gone, the item has been sold. This should tell you a lot about how popular those products are. If you notice the same item or a similar one is up for sale a day or so later, this person is reselling, and that niche is therefore quite in demand.

Overall, the most important points to take away from this book are:

- Craigslist is a local classified ads site, which allows you to buy and sell from people within your local area
- Listing an item for sale is completely free, however, you will pay a small amount if you are listing for a property, a job, or certain services, e.g. holistic
- Once you sell the item, you do not pay any fees, which makes Craigslist preferable to large sites, such as eBay
- You do not need to package or post items to buyers, as the collection is done via a meetup

- Safety is vital when it comes to meeting a buyer or a seller, and you should always exercise caution and common sense, e.g. never go to someone's house or have anyone come to your house
- There are certain scams which might take place on Craigslist, and knowing about these ahead of time, and using your gut, will help you to avoid any unfortunate circumstances
- Always be honest when selling items on Craigslist
- Always list your item in the right category, to avoid missing a sale because the product was too hard to find. Remember, there are countless products for sale on Craigslist within any specific area, and nobody wants to look through all of them!
- When setting the price you want to sell a product for, always go around 2-3% higher, as the buyer is likely to try and negotiate the price with you anyway
- Ensure you take high-quality photographs of items as you post them, and if possible, post more than one photo to enhance the chances of a sale
- Never give out your bank details or any other financial information to a buyer or a seller. Only ever use cash, and if that isn't possible, PayPal as a last resort

These are the main points you should be more than aware of by this point in the book. Remember to start slow and keep your sales and purchases low cost as you begin your journey into making cash from Craigslist. As your experience and confidence grow, you can quickly increase your profit margin, but working slowly will allow you to gain the necessary knowledge and avoid any potential pitfalls that might otherwise come your way.

All that is left to say is 'good luck'!

Thank you for reading " The Smart Craigslist Guide ".

If you enjoyed this book and found this book helpful , please consider leaving a review, even if it's only a few lines; it would make all the difference and would be very much appreciated.

Steve Johnson